Rise Up: Be Resilient Like You're Running Out Of Time

By Ashley M. Stephenson

Disclaimers: This book is designed to provide information and motivation with regard to the subject matter covered. By its sale, neither the publisher nor the author is engaged in rendering psychological or other professional services. If expert mental health or psychological assistance is needed, the services of a professional should be sought.

The views or opinions represented are personal and belong solely to the author and do not represent those of individuals, institutions, or organizations that the author may or may not be associated with in professional or personal capacity unless explicitly stated.

Any views or opinions are not intended to malign any group, organization, company, individual, or religion.

Contents

Introduction

Resilience 101

Chapter 1

Why You Need Resilience:

The Benefits of Being Resilient

Are There Different Types Of Resilience?

Chapter 2

How To Develop and Promote Resilience:

Practical, Easy-to-implement and Effective Resilience Strategies

Chapter 3

Characteristics of Resilient People:

Good Resilient Abilities

Chapter 4

Applying Resilience:

How to Apply Resilience in Different Areas of Your Life

Resiliency in the Workplace

Resiliency in Leadership

Resiliency in Relationships

Resiliency in Dealing with Difficult People

Conclusion

Introduction

Failure, difficulty, and suffering are unavoidable parts of the human experience. We will all encounter unexpected events from time to time, and some may get us stuck in a slump. That's how the wheel of life turns.

It's easy to face life when everything is going smoothly, but when we encounter a major bump in the road, how can we react and adapt in a way that supports our general well-being?

A life that is worth living will undoubtedly face adversity.

Everyone has different ways of responding to adverse events. Some people become trapped in adversity, while others choose to rise and learn from difficult experiences. The psychological resources influence different ways of reacting to adversity that a person has.

In order to bounce back from hardship and move on from the inevitable challenges that will come our way in life, we need arguably the most valuable skill to have in life, resilience.

There's no guarantee that you won't face setbacks in life, but how you choose to deal with them is in your control.

No one ever says:

- *"I want to give up on my dreams."*
- *"I want to be miserable and full of regrets."*

Why do people not make such comments?

It's because we all know that the good things in life don't get handed to us on a silver platter, and to create the life of our dreams, we need to be as resilient as a microscopic creature that can survive 300-degree temperatures, up to 30-years without food or water, and even several days in space – the tardigrade.

Credit: Wholesome Memes; Herta Burbe©

- *What is resilience?*
- *Why is it important to have?*
- *Why do some people bounce back from adversity and misfortune?*
- *Why do others fall apart?*

If you've ever asked yourself any of these or related questions, this book will distill everything you would want to know about resilience into an easy-to-digest and easy-to-implement guidebook.

In this book, we'll examine resilience: what it is, why we need it, the different types of resilience, and how to develop it; so that we have the strength and determination to overcome adversity and to keep on moving forward towards our dreams and our goals.

Having and maintaining this trait is not very simple, as there is no magic "resilience pill." The key is lifestyle changes, which may initially be a bit daunting, but can better equip us to meet life's challenges head-on.

Now, I'm not an expert on resilience, and I won't pretend to be. Still, the life I have created for myself has provided me the opportunity to meet and observe people from different walks of life. Some of which can demonstrate high levels of resilience that many would only hope to see—those who know defeat, suffering, struggle, and loss—who have beat all odds and found their way out of those depths. How does this happen? These people have the ability to welcome change and difficulty as an opportunity for self-reflection, learning, and growing.

Within this book, you'll learn about the tools and techniques I've discovered—often learned from personal experience and from those inspirational people I've had the good fortune to meet—that create a resilient mindset.

Resilience 101

Socially, politically, and economically, the world we live in is one of perpetual change, challenge, and adversity—and all of it taking place at break-neck speed. A pervasive sense of uncertainty—even fear—is the result. Many perceive resilience as a way to cope, but resilience is more about managing one's energy in a new way for new times. When we lack resilience, we are effectively living in survival mode—relentlessly pushing on, yet unable to see a wider perspective, simply existing, in other words, in a state of reactivity as opposed to one of creativity.

Due to the unpredictability of life, there will always be joys and sorrows. We all have situations where things don't go our way, change is dumped upon us, or when the unexpected happens. How we approach these situations can often mean the difference between dusting ourselves off and moving on or being crushed by disappointment. Some of us will collapse under the stress and worry, while others who are able to handle these events will take them in stride and persist as if nothing occurred. Why is that? Do some people have a different outlook or possess skills that others don't? The chances are they are more resilient than others.

Resilience is one of those psychological concepts that can be hard to define, as it's both complex and multidimensional. Presumably, you likely have your own idea of what it means—maybe the ability to withstand hardship or to get back up after something knocks you down.

To understand what resilience is, we must understand what it is not. There is a mistaken image of how resilience can be defined. Having resilience does not mean that people do not *feel* pain, and it does not mean that resilient people are able to cope without asking for help. In fact, quite the opposite is true. Resilience does not eliminate stress or erase one's difficulties.

Those who are resilient don't see life through rose-colored glasses, as they still experience the emotional pain, grief, and sense of loss that comes after a tragedy, but their mental outlook allows them to work through such feelings and recover.

Additionally, resilience is not tenacity. It's not the ability to stick with a task no matter how difficult the task may be and to see it through. Instead, resilience gives people the strength to tackle problems head-on, overcome adversity, and move forward with their lives.

While certain factors make some individuals more resilient than others, resilience isn't necessarily a personality trait that only some people possess. Resilience does however involve behaviors, thoughts, and actions that anyone can learn and develop. Resilience is not just an inherent trait, it's a practice.

The word 'resilience' is derived from the present participle of the Latin word *resilire*, which can be defined as *"to spring back,"* or *"rebound."* Most commonly, resilience is defined as is the measure of our ability to welcome challenges, overcome adversity, and get back on track to achieve our goals. Resilience is confronting crises and difficult situations without getting overwhelmed by them.

I define resilience as the ability to bounce back from hardships and adversities and the ability to bounce forward in order to adapt to life's setbacks. It's the element that helps you recover from the difficulties or changes in the workplace, illnesses, disasters, the loss of a loved one, or any other challenge you might face at any point in your life.

Resilience is the key to a well-lived life and once developed, resilience will serve you well in every aspect of your life. It will allow you to draw upon your past experiences, both physical and emotional and help you manage and overcome difficult times. In fact, learning to be resilient can also help to make you stronger and with each challenge you encounter, you can develop new skills and new ways of dealing with life experiences.

When you lack resilience, there is a greater possibility to become overwhelmed by challenges, feel victimized, dwell on problems, and on occasion, turn to unhealthy coping mechanisms, such as catastrophizing – visioning and dwelling on the worst possible outcome, or substance abuse.

Resilience isn't an end goal, it's a mindset, a way of life. Building resiliency isn't something that occurs instantly overnight. Resilience takes time to build and can vary dramatically from one person to the next. Practicing the skills associated with resilience grows important competencies such as self-awareness, flexible thinking, strong relationships, purpose, and having a positive default. Resilience isn't about toughening up people—it's about empowering them.

The irony of resilience is that many people build resiliency to avoid challenges, mistakes and failures, when in reality, these difficult situations and the way you respond allow you to build resilience over time. You simply cannot be resilient without facing challenges. What you can do however, is continue building skills to improve your resilience.

Let's make one thing clear:

Although resilience may not be the answer to all your problems, being resilient gives you the ability to see past your problems, handle stress well, and find enjoyment in life, even if you're going through what may feel like a Herculean trial. It makes the process of finding solutions a lot easier.

How we view adversity and stress strongly affects how we succeed, and this is one of the most significant reasons why having a resilient mindset is so important.

The fact is that we're going to fail from time to time: it's an inescapable part of living that we misstep and occasionally fall flat on our faces.

If you feel like you are a bit more vulnerable to stress, or not as resilient as you would like to be, resilience is a skill you can learn and strengthen. By nurturing your resilience, this crammed guidebook with random insights and helpful tips will help you become stronger and more adaptable, even during the toughest of times.

Are you ready for that?

Well then, let's begin!

Chapter 1

Why You Need Resilience:

The Benefits of Being Resilient

All life is an experiment. The more experiments you make, the better. What if they are a little coarse, and you may get your coat soiled or torn? What if you do fail and get fairly rolled in the dirt once or twice? Up again, you shall never more be so afraid of a tumble."
-Ralph Waldo Emerson

Everyone is dealing with greater uncertainty, ambiguity, and change than ever before. Recent years have provided an amazing opportunity to explore the bounds of resilience and reflect deeply on the factors that can drain or replenish energy for each of us. The feelings of being mentally drained, angry, concerned, and frightened are understandable during these times, yet resilience can help you improve your well-being and steer through everyday challenges.

Our ability to respond to and cope with life is generally a direct reflection of how many challenges we've encountered. When we learn to respond to our circumstances more effectively, and especially through practice and repetition, we develop the character needed to get through life with more ease.

To echo the words of John Allen Paulo's:

> ***"Uncertainty is the only certainty in life, and knowing how to live with insecurity is the only security."***

Here are evocative reasons why being resilient can make all the difference in your life:

You need resilience for your general well-being

Your mind can have a positive or negative effect on your body. Because of this, part of resilience is how you think and the understanding of the importance of rationality and composure when dealing with stressful situations. Staying positive or finding balance when all hell seems to be breaking loose and nothing is going as planned is not easy. During these times, resilience enables you to overcome the misfortune and pick yourself up by the bootstraps and move forward when life takes you off course.

It's human nature to think negatively in a challenging situation, especially during an unpredictable one. Positive thinking and self-talk are not only good for our general health, they can influence our overall outlook on life.

Incorporating positive thinking and other healthy habits into your life is powerful because they autocorrect our lives in times of desperation. For instance, the more hopeless, sad, or desperate you feel, the more healthy habits can help improve your well-being. Exercise, healthy eating, taking supplements, getting fresh air, or speaking to a therapist, are all healthy distractions which are essential for self-care and in return, comes from meeting your needs, not denying them.

It takes something unique—resilience—to make it through moments when you feel like nothing is going your way, the world has stacked all the odds against you, or when everything you want seems to be coming to you in trickles. That maddening feeling can make throwing in the towel seem like the best thing in the world, but it's not!

In such moments, you need resilience!

Being resilient protects you from getting too overwhelmed by challenges and stress and from developing mental health problems, and it generally safeguards your well-being.

Stress is an all-too-common occurrence many are too familiar with. Not only is it unpleasant, but it can also have serious effects on your physical, emotional, and mental health. Whenever you face stress, whether it be the minor hassles of daily life or a major crisis that transforms your life, your brain and body go through a series of changes impacting how you react. When stress is prolonged, your immune system can become weakened, leaving you more susceptible to illness. Resilience—and the positive emotions it brings—works against that by promoting better mental health.

Resilience also supports healthy habits, behaviors, and health-promoting practices. For instance, if you have resilience, you may feel more encouraged to quit smoking, excessive drinking, or recreational drugs and replace these habits with healthier practices such as running, yoga, meditation, strength training, or even creating a solid support system. The latter habits help make your life better in many different ways. For instance, exercising improves your cardiovascular health, sleep quality, and general well-being.

Resilience helps you embrace change

There are many people who spend their entire lives fearing change. The prospect of facing change leaves them fearful of the unknown. Change always catches up to you though. Accepting the inevitability of change is one of the building blocks of resilience.

The reality is the world we live in is constantly changing and learning to roll with life's changes will lead to a happier and more fulfilling life. This doesn't mean ignoring sadness or frustration, you can acknowledge these feelings, but resilience allows you to move forward and focus your energy on what's important.

While I don't believe that people naturally resist change, people resist the pain associated with change and the fear of the unknown. Pain and suffering are undeniably real for everyone. Still, by resisting, we end up living a difficult life of pain and suffering because resistance makes it impossible to find comfort in the new form of 'chaos' brought about by change.

Using your resilience threshold means to become comfortable with the uncomfortable. To evolve, you must know that discomfort is a sign of growth. Comfort is something we all seek in life, whether it consists of staying familiar with a routine or staying close to what is well-known to us, avoiding the unknown and discomfort are things often too familiar to some.

Building and mastering resilience requires you to move out of your comfort zone and be comfortable in the land of the unknown. Doing this—being deliberately uncomfortable—requires you to work on your inner self by doing things like breaking bad habits, replacing your limiting beliefs, and learning how to turn stress and challenges into acquaintances you can use to your advantage. Your personal growth is beyond your comfort zone. You improve when your body or mind is stretched to its limits in a voluntary effort to accomplish something worthwhile.

When we are uncomfortable in our lives, it is often because life is demanding a better version of us. Though hardship and discomfort can seem as though they should be our enemy, they're actually our greatest ally, as both are deep and pervasive knowing that we are deserving, capable, and destined for more.

Once you start doing that, no amount of change will leave you feeling scared or uncomfortable. Instead, you will embrace change, seek it, love it, and work with it to achieve your dreams.

Resilience helps you achieve your dreams or goals

According to legend, Thomas Edison made thousands of prototypes of the incandescent light bulb before getting it right. And, since the prolific inventor was awarded more than 1,000 patents, it's hard to imagine him failing more than a handful of times in his lab.

One of his well-known quotes reads:

> *"I have not failed. I have just found 10,000 ways that won't work."*
> - Thomas Edison

Can you imagine the degree of resilience it took to continue trying something after failing thousands of times? Despite struggling with "failure" throughout his entire working life, Edison never let it get the best of him. Instead, he chose to remain positively resilient. All of these "failures" simply showed him how not to invent something. As it turned out, his resilience gave the world some of the most amazing inventions of the early 20th century, such as the phonograph, the telegraph, and the motion picture.

It's hard to imagine what our world would be like if Edison had given up after his first few failures. His inspiring story forces us to look at our own lives—do we have the resilience that we need to overcome our challenges? Or do we let our failures derail our dreams? And, what could we accomplish if we had the strength not to give up?

You must persist in the face of obstacles and failures. Demonstrating perseverance and commitment as you pursue a long-term goal or dream is the key to succeeding.

To achieve everything you've ever wanted, you must remain resiliently committed; only then shall you be able to see challenges as opportunities instead of threats or roadblocks to your success.

Resilience helps you to build an internal locus of control

Consider the following simple questions:

- *Does life happen to you or for you?*
- *Do you make your decisions based on personal guiding principles, or do external forces dictate the decisions you make?*

Your answers to these questions can determine how effectively you live your life and overcome challenges.

In the 1950's, psychologist Julian Rotter theorized that human behavior could be explained by whether a person has an internal or external *locus* (derived from "place" in Latin) of control. Dr. Rotter theorized that those with an external locus of control believe that their behavior is guided by luck and other external factors. While those with an internal locus of control believe that their own actions and decisions guide their behavior. People however, don't fit into one extreme or the other, rather the two categories represent the opposite ends of a continuum.

People who depend on the external locus of control have difficulty bouncing back from life's setbacks. They tend to believe that an external force determines their life's direction. Hence, they tend to feel powerless and often feel victimized, while having difficulty accepting responsibility for their own lives, leaving them more prone to stress, anxiety, and depression.

On the other hand, those with an internal locus of control tend to thrive in the midst of change. They see themselves as the masters of their own lives and fate and exhibit a greater control over their own behaviors, while seeking to learn as much as possible. They know that they are in control of the most important thing in their lives: themselves. Thus, they can get back on their feet when they get knocked down because they know how to control themselves and use challenges, stress, and adversities as springboards for success.

Resilient people understand that life happens—they know that suffering is a part of life—this doesn't mean that they welcome it into their lives, but when hard times come, they seem to know that suffering is a part of human existence.

In August 2019, comedian and television host Stephen Colbert participated in a particularly moving interview with journalist Anderson Cooper, in which the topic of grief was discussed. As both men have experienced loss in their lives, they shared some of their experiences in the interview. While Colbert explained how his upbringing pushed him towards comedy, Cooper questioned how he learned to accept tragedy as a way of life.

During their conversation, Colbert replied:

> ***"…It's a gift to exist, and with existence comes suffering. There's no escaping that."***

While some would argue it's a struggle to exist, resilient people can agree with Colbert in reframing the struggle as a gift. They know they will experience hard times and failures, but as they see it, these times are not something to dwell on, rather as an opportunity to move forward and accept hard times and failures are all a part of life. Pain and suffering are keys to windows of opportunity— opportunity for something new, opportunity to improve, opportunity to see things differently. Without pain and suffering, there is no way to life. A resilient life isn't one lived on the sidelines for fear of failure. It's one that dares to tests our limits. Failure in life isn't an excuse, it's a challenge to keep progressing forward.

The internal locus of control that comes with being resilient can help you become the driver of your destiny; it can help you create a life of your choosing. Though you cannot always control what you feel, you can control how you respond, and in that response, you can find your freedom.

Are There Different Types Of Resilience?

Discussions about resilience often involve the term: "emotional resilience," which is our individual capacity to cope with adversity in life. The term further refers to managing the emotional impact of stresses, difficulties, and traumas experienced in life.

The truth is that we develop different types of emotional resiliencies at varied points in our lives. These include:

Inherent Resilience

Inherent resilience is inborn, natural resilience. It refers to dealing with routine challenges that life brings. It's your human nature and life force that we can consider generational because your folks pass it down to you in your DNA. Therefore, if your parents are resilient, your chances of being a naturally more resilient person are higher.

This inherent or natural resilience functions to protect, inform, and guide us as we discover and explore the world. It takes credit for all childhood activities like learning to play, taking risks, and testing boundaries.

This type of resilience is prominent in children below the age of seven. However, it often persists throughout life, provided that nothing, for example, traumatic experiences, disrupts the child's development. Adaptive resilience, discussed below, can also be bolstered by inherent resilience.

Adaptive Resilience

Adaptive resilience is the ability to recover from adversity, adapt to change, and thrive. It helps builds the capacity to be productive, resourceful, and creative while dealing with changing circumstances or disruptive forces. This resilience develops when challenging circumstances force you to learn and adapt from things such as the hustle and bustle of looking for a job after getting fired, ending a relationship and finding the strength to build your confidence once again, or dealing with a particularly stressful work situation over an extended period of time.

By developing or strengthening your adaptive resilience, you gain the courage to face your fears and adapt your attitude to allow you to focus on the possibilities even in the worst of times. The tougher the situation, the tougher you become.

Adaptive resilience is something we learn and develop by going through difficult experiences. This type of resilience is vital because it helps us manage challenges, pain, and life's many stressors. By fostering the courage to deal with the unforeseen and adversity freely, your adaptive resilience can be strengthened, which can help you have clarity in the face of challenges and shift your mindset to view things from a different perspective.

Adaptive resilience requires much more than learning new techniques and skills, it requires a shift in your way of being and the way you engage with the world around you. When you enter into the realm of adaptive resilience, you not only learn how to handle stress and build better relationships; you also learn how to assess your response to problems in order to create new possibilities and sustainable outcomes.

Learned Resilience

Life doesn't get easier or more forgiving, but we can get stronger and more resilient. Like adaptive resilience, we build learned resilience over time through challenges. The main difference between learned and adaptive resilience is that you can use the lessons learned from difficult past experiences to activate learned resilience. You can draw on and use learned resilience whenever you're facing a difficult experience or under stressful times. We know that life is not what happens to us with learned resilience, but what happens within us.

Learned resilience is how you can learn to grow and develop your ability to manage difficult times. It also helps you find ways to draw on an inner strength you never knew you had when you need it the most.

As learned resilience is the most highly effective type of resilience you can possess, this book is filled will strategies meant to help you develop and improve learned resilience.

Chapter 2

How To Develop and Promote Resilience:

Practical, Easy-to-implement and Effective Resilience Strategies

"What seem to us bitter trials are often blessings in disguise."
-Oscar Wilde

Have you ever tried to build muscles or get lean?

If you have, you know that doing so takes time, intentionality, and unbreakable consistency. The longer you keep at it, the strong and bigger your muscle becomes.

Building resilience works similarly: it takes time, intentionality, and consistency. Developing and strengthening your resilience is a personal journey and the cornerstone of success and happiness in life. It's the element that helps you believe that you are strong and capable of surviving any situation.

Demonstrating resilience doesn't necessarily mean that you have not suffered difficulty, distress, or adversity in life, and it doesn't mean you have not experienced emotional pain or sadness. The road to resilience is often paved with emotional stress and strain. The good news is that the more adversity we experience, the more opportunity we have to develop our resilience. In order to get there, we need to continually grow through positive and negative experiences. Developing a greater level of resilience won't prevent dreadful or stressful things from happening, but it can help reduce the level of disruption that stress can have and the time it takes to recover.

If you want to build a strong sense of emotional resilience, you have to commit to it for the long haul. Although it takes time, the rewards are well worth the effort.

To develop learned resilience, you should focus on these core components:

- *Connections,*

- *Wellness,*

- *Healthy/positive thinking, &*

- *Finding meaning or purpose in life.*

Let discuss each of these components and strategies you can use to develop each:

Building positive connections/relationships

Often times, when we experience stress or trauma, the most natural response is to retreat into an isolated place, building imaginary walls that shut everyone out.

When your view of the world gets shaken and things become unpredictable, going to a place that makes you feel safe or a place that can rejuvenate your spirit might seem the best thing to do.

However, although giving ourselves some personal space and time can help with emotional healing, self-isolation is the opposite of what we need to do to foster resilience.

Emotional strength, coping, and pushing through stress and challenges are all beneficial in fostering resilience. You can't do that if, when you face a challenge, you give in to the first instinct to self-isolate or give up.

An essential key to building resilience is connecting with people that can validate, empathize, and understand your feelings and experiences. One of the most profound experiences we can have in our lives is the connection we have with other human beings. By building positive relationships with others, we will feel more supported, supportive, happier, and connected. In addition to feeling more fulfilled in our day-to-day life, positive and supportive relationships will help us to feel healthier, happier, and more satisfied.

You can build connections by:

Prioritizing building your relationships

Resilience has a lot to do with leaning on the people around you and developing strong, supportive connections. Our brains need social support to function optimally. Connection with others releases oxytocin which calms your mind and reduces stress. When you create relationships with understanding and empathetic people, they can remind you that you are not alone when dealing with a stressful experience. Reliable, trustworthy, and supportive relationships can offer the emotional support you need to manage stress, overcome difficulties, and build your resilience.

Everyone can benefit in their lives by having people they can lean on. Building a tight-knit circle of people you can trust and who respect you is a key part of strengthening your resilience and weathering difficult times. By focusing on creating relationships with compassionate people you can trust, your feelings can be validated and your resilience can be strengthened.

The pain experienced from difficult or traumatic events may cause some people to isolate themselves, something we all occasionally do because it's part of our human nature.

However, it is crucial and way better to accept help and support from people that love and care about you. Positive relationships and friendships are known to reduce stress, increase your happiness, and even increase your lifespan.

Prioritize genuinely connecting with people and building trust and true friendship with others. Surround yourself with people who make you hungry for life, touch your heart, and nourish your soul. When you do, the people in your life will support you whenever you are experiencing a difficult time.

Join a group

Besides intimate relationships, group activities—whether faith-based groups, civic groups, or other support-based local organizations—can help you develop resilience.

That's because:

When you interact and talk to people who have or are going through the same traumatic events you are, it becomes easier to share your pain, feel like you are not alone, and feel encouraged to keep going until you get over the stress.

Find a local or online group that can offer you support, a sense of hope and purpose, or even joy amid a stressful time. The type of group you should settle down in should not be judgmental. It should empower you, improve your coping skills, give you a sense of adjustment, and help you reduce distress, depression, anxiety, and fatigue.

Foster wellness

Wellness means being healthy, feeling good, taking good care of yourself, and ensuring you achieve your highest level of well-being, including your physical, mental, and emotional health.

Fostering wellness helps build resilience because when you take good care of yourself before and during challenging times, it enhances your ability to manage and make it through challenging situations.

Individual resilience incorporates your physical health, as well as your emotional and mental health and your well-being. These all contribute to enabling you to adapt to different forms of adversity – often characterized as an inner strength.

Now that you know how personal wellness fosters emotional resilience, below are potent wellness approaches you can use to become more resilient:

Take good care of your body

Self-care sounds like a cliché, a popular buzzword you've probably heard 10,000 times. It's unique for each person and can be understood in many different ways. In its simplest form, the term refers to our ability to function effectively in the world while dealing with and conquering the multiple challenges of daily life with a sense of energy, vitality, and confidence.

Although the term has become a buzzword, the actual practice is not; it's a legitimate practice that improves your mental health and fosters resilience. That's because stress is as much physical as it is emotional.

Embracing self-care practices that promote a healthier lifestyle, things like eating nutritious foods, getting adequate sleep, drinking enough water, and exercising regularly, can help you develop mental and physical strength.

For example, regular exercise can help strengthen your physical body, making it more resilient to stress, and in the process, helping limit and reduce the mental toll of conditions like stress, fear, anxiety, depression, etc. The stress of exercise helps us adapt to the stress we will feel when life challenges us.

You might be wondering how sleeping enough, having a consistent exercise routine, or eating healthy foods relates to building resilience.

As it turns out, the amount of sleep you get directly influences how you experience stress. When you fail to get adequate sleep, you experience small stressors more intensely than someone who gets sufficient sleep regularly.

When you deny your body enough sleep, you consequently deprive your brain of the time it needs to do certain functions that strengthen your neuroplasticity, which is the brain's capacity to adapt and change by building new neural pathways. When you get enough sleep, you give your brain time to rebuild itself, giving it the ability to cope with difficulties, challenges, or stressors.

Unfortunately, stress can interfere with the amount of sleep you get. For instance, people with a lot of stress report struggling to fall asleep. The good news is that how much sleep you get—and the quality—is in your control because you can control your circadian rhythm, the internal clock regulating activities like sleep.

You can do this by getting enough sunlight during the day, exercising, and avoiding using your phone or other electronic devices at night, and going to bed and waking up around the same time every single day.

Exercising can also help you build your resilience. Moderate to regular exercise decreases cortisol levels, which is beneficial, as cortisol is the hormone responsible for stress. Exercise also supports a regulated sleep-wake cycle, which promotes healthy sleep. Exercising for 20-30 minutes per day or going out for a walk can reduce cortisol levels, reduce stress, anxiety, and increase your daytime energy.

When we feel stressed, many of us cope by indulging in stress eating, eating whatever is quick and available, often high carb, high fat, or high sugar foods. We've all heard the saying "you are what you eat." Well, there's some truth to it and regardless of how good these foods may taste, food choices can either build or deplete your resilience. Stress eating will be quick to do the latter.

Eating a diet high in Omega-3 fatty acids, fresh fruits and vegetables, nuts, whole grains, fish, and reduced red meat and refined sugars is beneficial to your well-being. Integrating these foods into your meal plans improves your health and can help you become more resilient because making healthy food choices fosters self-discipline.

For instance, fruits and vegetables have antioxidants that reduce inflammation caused by stress and unhealthy eating. Using food to your advantage is a type of literacy many of us were unfortunately not taught, but building health is about nutritional knowledge and improving habits. The more healthy foods you incorporate into your diet, the more strength you'll have to get through the difficult times.

Practice mindfulness

Mindfulness, as a concept, can seem rather vague. The term can be best described as the practice of being aware in the present moment without judgment or preconceptions and gratitude for the present.

Practicing mindfulness allows you to distance yourself from your emotions. For instance, you might say to yourself, *"I'm angry with Chanel."* This statement implies that you are *feeling* your emotions. A mindful approach might be to say, *"I am experiencing anger,*" allowing you to *be aware* of what you are feeling. By objectifying your emotions, they cease to have control over you. Mindfulness allows you to bring yourself back to what is happening now, and not stress about what could happen.

Mindfulness-based practices like journaling, yoga, and spiritual practices like prayer and meditation can also help you connect with yourself, cope, and be hopeful, which are crucial in dealing with situations that require resilience.

Mindfulness does not stop difficult emotions; it helps you relate more wisely with your emotions. It enables you to see life more clearly and respond appropriately to your challenging situations instead of reacting to them.

When practicing mindfulness, remember to remain calm, see things as they are instead of thinking of what they may be, be compassionate and courageous with yourself, and connect with your senses.

Being calm helps your brain see clearly and allows you to solve the problem or the challenge you are facing effectively. Being compassionate with yourself by actively noticing and recognizing that you are in difficulty helps you be kind to yourself, which helps you comfort yourself.

Don't let your mind believe worrisome thoughts that try to convince you that things will never be "normal or good" again. Replace such negative thoughts with positive ones that give you the faith to believe that you shall triumph over difficulty. Connect with your senses by feeling your breath, the air as it touches your skin, and your body as it is right now.

Lastly, be courageous and face challenges head-on, even when you're fearful. It's easy to avoid thinking about the traumatic event, but you need to see it and feel it as it is to get over it. An approach to building resilience that works for one person might not work for another. Once your mind knows and gets used to pain caused by stressful events, it will become much easier to see past it and move on with life.

Here is a mindful exercise that can help build your resilience:

- Find a quiet place; it can be a quiet room or anywhere else where you won't be disturbed or distracted by anyone or anything.

- Close your eyes, breathe slowly, and focus your attention on every inhale and exhale.

- Whenever you get distracted, simply return to your breathing, using the breath like your mindfulness anchor.

- While still focusing on your breath, allow all your thoughts, feelings, beliefs, and senses to enter your awareness as you think about your external stressful situation.

Then ask yourself:

- *"What are the facts about the difficult situation I am experiencing?"*

- *"What are my thoughts, feelings, and emotions about this situation?"*

- *"How am I responding right now?"*

- *"How should I respond to get past the difficult situation?"*

After several practices, this exercise will get you into a calm and reflective state of mind. You will find internal peace and begin to see things more clearly.

You will deconstruct, recontextualize, and reframe the original feelings and reactions caused by stress, depression, and anxieties, and you will find a way to appreciate and embrace them without being their victims. In so doing, your resilience will be getting stronger and stronger with time.

Avoid negative outlets

Stress affects people in different ways – or at least, different people respond to it very differently. For some, it rolls off quickly, and they rebound in a reasonable amount of time. For others, it "sticks" and it takes a longer amount of time to recover, if they ever recover. This is because people's mental "resilience" varies enormously.

For some people, they may repeatedly think about what could have been done differently in the past, or how they may mess up again in the future. Some people will ruminate on events because they believe that thinking about hardships over and over will help them solve them. These negative thought cycles only cause one to get caught up in their thoughts, rather than taking the necessary actions needed to move forward.

By taking a behavioral break – forcing yourself to think positively on a memory or redirecting your mind elsewhere, you are forcing your brain to switch gears, thus breaking the negative thought cycle.

<u>Transform pain into power</u>

Resilience starts with the adversity, pain, or challenge you have been subjected to being converted into powerful nourishment that can bring new opportunities. Plain and simple, pain equals power.

The first step to transform pain into power is to allow yourself to feel those heavy emotions you are experiencing. The longer you pretend not to feel them, self-medicate, or shove negative emotions aside, the longer they will float in the abyss of your thoughts.

Once you allow yourself to digest what you are feeling, you can access where the pain is coming from and from there, you will see that there is a valuable lesson to be learned like all life's experiences. At that time, you can turn your newfound knowledge into action and you will begin to see that gradual shift from pain to power.

Find a purpose

Purpose is a recognition that we belong to and serve something bigger than ourselves. Our purpose in life helps to shape the mindset and attitude we have toward others and the events we experience. Everyone has a purpose that drives their actions. For some, that purpose may be financial-driven. For others, that purpose may be being a great parent. Regardless of that purpose, there's always some reason behind the things that we do.

Resilient people can adapt to challenges without compromising their sense of purpose. They know when it's appropriate to reach out and also when to reach in. In other words, they know how to seek support, as well as how to manage their own resources, time, and energy. More than anything else, resilient people recognize and are driven by a purpose greater than themselves.

Finding a purpose, your reason for existence, or your value to the world and other people, can help you stay strong and be resilient. Remember, if we want to be resilient, we need something to be resilient for.

Here're some strategic approaches you can use to live a purposeful life:

Help others

Whether it's volunteering at a local homeless shelter or supporting a friend or family member in their own time of need, you can develop a sense of purpose, foster self-worth, connect deeper with other people, and tangibly help others in need. All of these activities can empower you to become more resilient.

Helping and supporting others can also give you hope, because when you feel like you have done something valuable for someone else, and because of you, that person is now in a much better place, it can leave you feeling more valuable. Feeling valuable is enough to counter the stress of dealing with a difficult situation.

Be proactive

Resilient people experience anger, just like everyone else; they just don't allow it to consume them. We all have this ability to not allow anger to become pent up inside us and to move on. It can feel good to nurture the self-pity, the anger, and the blame. On the contrary, it's more beneficial to acknowledge and accept your feelings and emotions during difficult times. However, it's just as important to find a way to be more proactive in life by asking yourself:

"What can I do about this stressful event in my life?"

Asking yourself this question helps to foster self-discovery.

If the problem seems too big to tackle, it may be helpful to work on it as a goal by breaking it down into manageable pieces, creating a plan, and solving one issue at a time.

Being proactive can help you become more resilient because it makes it easier to realize that hard times don't last when you keep doing something about them or moving forward with your life.

Additionally, taking the initiative will remind you that amid chaos, you can still find a way to muster motivation and purpose, which will increase your likelihood of rising to the occasion when facing another challenging experience.

Establish goals

While crises may seem daunting or insurmountable, you must view these situations in a logical way and set reasonable goals to deal with the situation.

When you become overwhelmed by a situation, take a step back to reassess what is before you. By brainstorming possible solutions, you can break down the barriers and establish goals.

You have goals in your life, right?

If not, you must change that **IMMEDIATELY** by writing down what you want to accomplish, whether or not you think it's realistic. Next, note what you need to do in order to get there, no matter how small it may seem, as that will enable you to move closer to your goal. Acknowledge your strengths and record the qualities of self-motivated or self-assured people you admire.

Don't be stressed by things that seem unachievable; work on what you can accomplish now with the resources and time you have right now. Then make a plan of doing the other things at some other time, and ensure that you do those things in the times set for them.

Working on your goals gives you purpose. It reminds you that you have bigger and more important things than the setbacks or challenges you're facing. A goal is like a compass: it gives your life direction.

Reframe setbacks as self-discovery opportunities

Resilient people recognize the futility—consciously or unconsciously—of fretting over something that can't be changed. They also look for lessons that can be learned from the setback.

They recognize that one way to grow or mature is by surviving a difficult event, something many resilient and successful people conquer themselves. For instance, after a challenging event or tragedy, many people have reported having a greater sense of strength and better relationships, even when feeling vulnerable.

Many people want success, but few want to put in the work through the rejections and disappointments. Resilient people appreciate the process and don't allow these external hurdles to ruin their internal dedication. They continue looking for opportunities.

You, too, can look for the opportunities behind your challenges, failures, or tragedies. Think of what good can come out of it and what you have learned from it. When looked at from a different angle, the thing stressing you now can help increase your sense of self-worth and heighten your appreciation of life.

Embrace healthy, positive thoughts

Positivity is one of the most effective ways to develop resiliency. That's because when you're deliberately looking for what's positive or good about a situation, you're not focusing on how bad things are. The mindset and the attitude you have while approaching a problem can make a difference in how resilient you are when dealing with a setback or troublesome circumstance.

Expressing anger or anxiety is not necessarily bad; however, allowing either to influence your decisions is not effective. With positivity, it strengthens a can-do, growth mindset that helps you believe in your ability to learn the skills you need to learn to develop effective solutions to challenges. A growth mindset pattern of thinking experiences failure as temporary, criticism as a guide for growth, and problems as opportunities.

Fortunately, developing positivity is not too challenging for the committed spirit. Here're some hacks you can use to develop healthy, positive, growth-focused thoughts:

Keeping things in perspective

As the saying goes, don't make a mountain out of a molehill. Even when facing challenging events, try to consider the stressful situation in a broader context and work to keep a long-term perspective. The way we view a setback or difficult situation can either make the crisis worse in our mind or minimize it.

Your thought process plays a significant role in how resilient you will be when facing challenges and setbacks. Looking at a problem from different angles and thinking outside the box, allows yourself to widen your perspective knowing that you are growing towards empowerment.

Habitually try to identify any irrational thoughts that come to mind, like the tendency to catastrophize difficulties, thinking the world is against you, or God is punishing you in some way.

Once you notice such thoughts, replace them with positive ones by adopting a more balanced and realistic thought pattern. Remind yourself that you are not alone, not the first to go through such a traumatic event, and you won't be the last one. By gaining a sense of control over negative thoughts, they stop being so unnerving.

Whatever you're facing, others have already been there, believed in themselves, and conquered it. When you are dealing with feelings of hopelessness, remind yourself that it's still possible to win. This is the beginning of resilience. Things will always happen in life; what matters is how you deal with them.

Your future depends on how you deal with your current challenges. As such, when facing a setback or tragedy, learn to change how you interpret and respond to it. In doing so, you will notice negative thoughts come and go, but you'll have the skills to handle them and to remind yourself that the best possible outcome is just as likely to occur as the worst possible outcome. Instead of seeing a challenging situation as an insurmountable problem, try reframing it as a challenge you are capable of overcoming.

Accept change

Accepting that change is inevitable is critical to developing resiliency. Developing the trait of resilience helps us not only survive change, but also learn, grow, and thrive when dealing with changes. Flexibility and learning how to be more adaptable helps one be better equipped in responding to difficult situations.

As mentioned earlier, change is the only certain thing about life. Once you learn and accept that, everything else will become easier to handle.

When it calls for it, don't hesitate to accept that a goal you'd given all your focus and energy is no longer attainable due to adverse situations in your life. Once you accept that, you won't struggle to change the goal and find a different purpose and target.

Accepting that you can't control or change everything helps you focus more on the things you can control and change. Some aspects of life are simply out of your control. Acknowledging and accepting this doesn't make you weak; it makes you strong. You can look at change as a challenge rather than a threat and control what you focus on and how long you allow yourself to suffer.

When you focus on the external world—particularly when blame enters the picture—you run into trouble. When starting with yourself, you can focus on your own reactions and your own ability to influence events. Expect things to work out. You can't change what happens, but you can change how you feel about it.

Resilient people move forward with their lives. They often utilize difficult events as an opportunity to branch out in new directions, while learning to adapt and thrive. On the other hand, people lacking resilience may get crushed by abrupt change and stuck trying to change the unchangeable and control the uncontrollable.

Maintain a positive outlook

Resilient people tend to maintain a positive, realistic outlook and cope with stress effectively. They don't dwell on the negative and instead look for opportunities in bleak situations. While doing such, they remind themselves that what they are facing is only temporary and they have overcome setbacks before and can do so again. A positive outlook enables us to expect that good things can and will happen in our lives.

To maintain a positive outlook, it may take gradual, small changes in your outlook on life and careful self-evaluation. Having confidence in your own ability to cope with life's stresses can play an important role in maintaining a positive outlook and building resilience for the future.

Often times, when things go bad, we get stuck thinking about the negative outcomes. Although it's challenging to have a positive outlook when things are going against you, being resilient calls on you to find a way to develop a positive outlook because an optimistic outlook empowers you to believe that there is still good to come.

By cultivating a mindset, which ultimately involves a desire to be open to change, things will start to feel like they're going your way when you believe that you can accept change for yourself. Everyone has a desire to have a positive life and to be happy, so cultivate a perspective that supports your desire.

Resilient people focus on what they can learn from the experience. You, too, can learn to focus on the positive and adopt a more positive outlook by visualizing what you want instead of worrying about what you fear. Then, look for ways to make your visualization a reality.

Learn from the past

Look back at what or who helped the last time you faced a struggle. What was it that helped you get through it and be hopeful again? You can use this knowledge to respond effectively to your current difficult situation.

Remind yourself of where you have been, how you managed, where you found the strength to carry on, and then ask yourself what you learned from those past experiences and how you can use them now. You can learn from the past through your mistakes and struggles. Every challenging event has the power to teach you something important.

When something bad happens, we tend to relive the event in our heads, repeatedly rehashing the pain. Learn to avoid this cycle by changing the narrative of your story with something more positive and optimistic. Learn to face your fears instead of avoiding them.

Fostering optimism does not mean ignoring the problem in order to focus only on positive outcomes. It means understanding that setbacks are temporary and that you have the skills and abilities to combat the challenges you face.

Be kind and compassionate to yourself and engage in mindful practices like meditation, yoga, journaling, and getting enough sleep. Eventually, you will realize that you are the strongest person you know and that you can get over anything life throws at you.

Chapter 3

Characteristics of Resilient People:

Good Resilient Abilities

"Courage is being scared to death—and saddling up anyway."
-John Wayne

In chapters one and two, we learned the benefits of being a resilient person and strategies you can use to become more resilient.

In this chapter, we'll look at characteristics you can use to gauge your progress towards being a more resilient person.

Resilient people have the following characteristics:

Resilient people practice detachment

Resilient people acknowledge difficult situations, keep calm and evaluate things rationally so they can make a plan and act.

When you become resilient, you will understand the separation between who you are and the causes of your temporary suffering. You'll become aware that the stress or trauma is just a part of your story, not your permanent identity.

Getting to a point where you feel like your mistakes, stressors, challenges, and setbacks do not define you is the hallmark of a growing sense of resilience. Once you get to that point, you'll be able to focus more on becoming who you are and working on your dreams with full confidence.

Problem-solving skills

Resilient people have well-developed problem-solving skills and engage in accurate, flexible thinking. They don't allow themselves to become defeated by negativity, which allows them to move forward and look for a solution to the problem. Those who are resilient believe that they are in control of some aspects of the situation and can facilitate a more positive outcome. Since they are emotional and mentally strong, they can detect the cause of the problem and see above the tragedies.

Thanks to this inclination, when a crisis emerges, they can spot the solution that can lead to a more positive outcome. They can be calm when handling their emotions and are rational when looking at problems, which is very important when envisioning a successful solution.

Resilient people are willing to sit in silence

Resilient people don't need distractions like television, gossiping, indulging in risky behavior, stress-eating, or other typical, ineffective, unhealthy coping strategies used by people overwhelmed by stress and trauma.

Resilient people are comfortable with their thoughts because they can watch them detachedly. They can watch negative, fearsome thoughts without reacting to them. They're comfortable with who they are and the thoughts they have.

They identify as survivors, not victims

When facing a crisis, resilient people don't look at themselves as victims. They recognize they are only a victim if they're currently being victimized in an exact moment. Anyone can be a victim of any given event, but nobody is a permanent victim unless they choose to be. Beyond that, you're only a victim if you choose to label yourself as such. Resilient people try to avoid negative thinking at all costs. Instead, they see themselves as survivors; they look for opportunities attached to a situation and find a way to resolve the problem as soon as they can. Even in situations that seem unavoidably dark, they remain focused on a positive outcome.

Those with a victim's mindset tend to hold on to negative events and accept defeat. Resilient people, however, choose to fight back. The resilient have misfortunes, just as everyone else, but those misfortunes never become part of their identity. They simply choose not to let misfortune change them unless it's for the better.

Being human means both positive and negative things will happen to you. If you experience a series of consecutive setbacks, taking a look at your own actions and behaviors would be a resilient approach for handling the setbacks. Might there be something you're doing that is bringing on the misfortune? If not, life happens. Know that the setback is only temporary, things always improve, and continue staying on course to the best of your ability.

Simply waiting for a problem to resolve itself only prolongs the crisis. Instead, start working on resolving the issue immediately, even if there isn't a fast or simple solution. Focus your attention on the progress, while realizing you are in control.

Resilient people are skilled in where they direct their attention. They have a habit of focusing on the things they can change, and somehow, learning to accept the things that they cannot. This is a vital, learnable skill for resilience. As humans, we're good at noticing the negatives. We are hardwired for that negative. Negative emotions tend to stick to us like sap from a tree, where positive emotions bounce off us like a trampoline.

In other words, resilient people don't ask why, they ask how. Resilient people don't diminish the negative, but use their energy to understand how they can change a situation or get out of a crisis. That's why they always end up winning.

Resilient people do not find it a challenge to ask for help

Arguably, most of us were raised in a society that perceives vulnerability as weakness, that rewards us for being 'self-reliant' and never asking for help. When in reality, vulnerability is the entry point to courage, innovation, empathy, and connection, all of which we need now more than ever. Although vulnerability may feel like weakness, it looks like courage to everyone else. Resilient people know that they should not suffer alone when someone else can help them find the needed solution.

Although there are resourceful when finding solutions to their problems, resilient people also know the importance of asking for help when things get difficult.

That's why resilient people are not afraid to call on someone they can confide in, should it be a mentor, therapist, friend, or family member, someone caring and supportive, who can listen and provide possible feedback or solutions to your problems. They also read books about self-improvement and research the solutions they need to move forward.

They don't take things personally

When you take something personally, you amplify its power. Sometimes we're on the wrong end of an event or action that causes us difficulty processing what occurred and the personal factor can amplify such events. Other times, we're caught up in an event that occurred, but it is now a personal attack on us. The difference between a personal attack and a non-personal attack is that a non-personal attack could happen to anyone. It's not because it's you that caused it to happen, it's just how the world (and the people in it) can be. Because of this, many times, we get to choose what we will take personally.

Taking things personally however does produce negative emotions and negative emotions decrease our resiliency.

Resilient people choose not to take most things personally.

They don't give up

The most impactful thing resilient people do is adapt and when their old ways can no longer support them, they reinvent.

Resilient people do not lose faith in a better tomorrow. They have a way of motivating themselves to keep going until changes take effect—remembering that change is inevitable. Some are invigorating; some are devastating. The key is how well we are able to cope with life's surprises.

A resilient person won't leave things to fate or expect things to happen as planned or intended. They know that things don't always pan out, and because of it, they're persistent, patient, and dedicated in their ways. When their main plan fails to work out, they develop another one and keep going until they finally find the answer they need— exactly what Edison did.

To be resilient, you must understand that the objective is to use what hits you to change your trajectory positively.

Life is not all rainbows and unicorns. Sometimes you will feel broken, depressed, forgotten, but persist anyway. We all need something to struggle against and to struggle for.

Once you master resilience, you will begin to develop such characteristics. You will learn to persist in the face of struggle, not for egoist purposes, but for the greater good and for the cultivation of your best self.

In order to continuously work on self-improvement, you will need to apply resilience in many different

areas of your life. Let us look at some of these areas
in the next chapter.

Chapter 4

Applying Resilience:

How to Apply Resilience in Different Areas of Your Life

"Beware: for I am fearless, and therefore powerful."
-Mary Wollstonecraft Shelley

Here's how you can apply your developing resiliency skills in different areas of life:

Resiliency in the Workplace

While resiliency is an essential life skill, it is extremely vital in the world of business. Workplaces are stressful environments full of countless challenges that test a person's tenacity. In our workplaces, stress levels, anxiety, and burnout are on the increase, with higher workloads, decreased budgets, challenging demands, and limited hours. These are all-pervasive impediments to our mental health. The ability to deal with such problems is what makes up workplace resiliency.

At work, resilience usually manifests as a company's or organization's ability to adapt quickly to changing trends and disruptions while still maintaining continuous business operations and safeguarding people, assets, and brand equity.

Business resilience goes beyond recovering from a disaster. It helps organizations adapt to change and serve as a building block for agility and sustained performance. It also involves adopting post-disaster strategies that can help stem future disasters, avoid costly downtime, vulnerabilities, and find a way of maintaining business operations in the face of unexpected challenges.

To build resilience in the workplace, you must ensure you have a clear vision and goals that everyone understands and adheres to, preserving workflows and ensuring that people still keep giving their best efforts in surviving the unexpected event.

Workplaces need individuals, leaders, and teams who are able to survive and thrive in the face of challenges.

To build resilience at work, you can focus on:

1. Positivity

By taking a positive stance at work, you can adapt to adversity and hold on to a sense of control over your work environment.

2. Emotional Insight

By developing and strengthening emotional insight, you can improve your resilience at work. Insight is related to emotional intelligence and individuals who possess insight have a level of awareness about the full range of emotions they experience, from negative to positive. Developing your emotional intelligence can also help develop your interpersonal skills, which can help navigate challenging situations to be less stressful.

3. Balance

By achieving a healthy work-life balance, you can improve your resilience. We've all heard about the equilibrium between personal life and professional work and we all have our own thoughts of what a healthy work-life balance entails, but in order to bounce back from stressful situations, employees need time to unwind and recuperate from work.

4. Meaning

Having a sense of meaning has been linked to developing resilience at work. This can be related to reducing vulnerability and the impact that adversity in the workplace has on you. Finding meaning in work, and feeling that you're playing an active role in contributing to something bigger than yourself, can help with the negative effects of stress.

5. Reflection

Becoming more reflective is another way to build resilience at work. Being in tune with your emotions and emotional reactions can serve to buffer against the effect of stress. Being aware of possible 'triggers' to stress can provide individuals with the opportunity to prepare and gather resources so they are better able to bounce back.

Resiliency in Leadership

In today's unpredictable landscape, leaders face new challenges, difficult decisions, and changing circumstances. To successfully navigate through times of uncertainty, you need to be adaptable, proactive, and, perhaps most importantly, resilient. In any organization, you see informal leaders and innovators emerge, and many of whom have had the privilege of being trained in the skills of resilience.

A resilient leader can see failure as a temporary setback that they can recover from quickly. Resilient leaders see the glass as half full rather than half empty. They see opportunity where others see problems, and view change as a positive rather than a negative. When setbacks occur, they look for the lessons to be learned rather than berating themselves or others for failing to achieve the goal. When faced with adversity, they remain focused on winning and keeping everyone else in the organization focused in that direction, as well.

Resiliency is one of the most important leadership traits because when facing workplace challenges, ambiguities, and turbulent periods, people look to their leader, expecting the guidance, motivation, wisdom, and knowledge they need to keep going on, stronger than ever.

Leaders need to take bold risks and make substantive decisions, knowing that people's lives depend on such big moves. Doing that is not simple, which is why, to function well during both the good and the bad times, leaders need resilience more than anything.

To be a resilient leader, you should:

1. Reframe How You Think

One of the most valuable tools in building resilience as a leader is to reframe a situation. This is where knowing what triggers your feelings of stress is helpful. Reframing requires examining a situation from a different perspective and asking what else could be going on. For example, if a valued employee resigns, you might focus on the loss, or you can choose to reframe it as a chance to hire new talent. As a resilient leader, you don't dwell on the negative and reframe your thinking to see a situation in a more positive light.

2. Communicate Effectively

In order for a leader to become and remain resilient, you need to bear in mind that everything you say or do will communicate something to someone and they only have so much capacity to communicate. Resilient leaders have the ability to think and communicate clearly and find solutions to complex situations even under duress. These leaders communicate their intentions to others while willing to help others understand a new strategy or direction. Effective communication helps others understand changes, expectations and new directions.

3. Help Those around You

As discussed earlier, helping others helps you find the purpose you need to get through changes. The most resilient leaders are not only focused on their own growth but also concerned with others' personal and professional development. Be bold when taking calculated risks and trying out new ideas that might work: no one will do it unless you do. By making an effort to help those around you, it will help build positive and trusting relationships with your teams in return.

4. Be Decisive

While resilient leaders are often championing change, they must also be able to make the decisions required to enact that change. Making decisions is always difficult because no person has all the information or understands all eventualities. However, until decisions are put in place, businesses cannot move forward. The most resilient leaders are effective at making decisions and moving forward.

5. Be Open to Feedback and Suggestions

Resilient leaders are open to feedback in order to demonstrate an effort to improve. These leaders are humble and coachable, as they exhibit a strong desire to improve their skills and abilities continuously. Analyzing feedback helps leaders see their behaviors and actions in a different light and can help them see where they need to change their approach when it comes to managing their teams.

Resiliency in Relationships

There is certainly a power in showing or expressing appreciation to those in your life. Whether it be a significant other, colleague, friend, or family member, gratitude is your power and your anchor when you feel upset or frustrated.

One of the favorable practices of highly successful and positive individuals is their relationship with gratitude. Expressing gratitude to a loved one not only makes the other person feel appreciated, but also puts into perspective how blessed you already are, which in return can boost your mood.

In order to enhance resilience in relationships, you must focus on having high-quality relationships with transparency, recognition, respect, and a sense of relatedness and belonging. Connecting with empathetic and understanding people can help remind you that you are not alone in the midst of difficulties.

To build resilience in relationships:

1. Be Available

Words might be comforting and reassuring, but they become meaningless without actions to back them up. In order to back up your words and avoid distrust in a relationship, making time for your partner requires availability and accessibility. Similarly, relationships need time and open communication to weed the inevitable hurts and resentments that occur. Consistently making time to bond on a physical, emotional, intellectual, and spiritual level is fundamental to deepen your relationship bond.

2. Be an Active Listener

The goal of being an active listener to listen deeply—acquiring information and understanding the person or the situation. A good place to start on what it means to be an active listener is to think about the difference between listening and hearing. Hearing is a passive physical process, which happens when sound hits our ears. Listening, on the other hand, is an action we consciously take. When we listen, we go beyond simply hearing words by giving our attention to what is being said. Active listening is about making a conscious decision to hear what the other person is saying. It's about being completely focused on others, through their words and their messages, without being distracted.

3. Be Empathetic

To have a healthy, strong relationship, it's important to feel deeply connected with the other person. The basis of emotional closeness in a relationship is empathy, the foundation of the experience of "we" rather than just "I" or "you." Empathy is necessary for intimacy, trust, and belonging. The ability to understand another person's experiences and emotions is a powerful relationship tool. In addition to promoting forgiveness, empathy is a hallmark of resilience. Empathetic people tend to be less selfish and have a genuine interest in the well-being of others.

4. Show Vulnerability

The best part of being human is the ability to connect with other humans, as we're automatically hardwired for it. The drive to connect is in all of us whether we acknowledge it or not. Without vulnerability, relationships struggle. Vulnerability is, "here I am with my frayed edges, secrets, fears, and dreams." Resilient individuals confide in one another and they respond compassionately to one another's disclosures. Vulnerability in relationships not only builds trust, closeness and a sense of belonging, but strong relationships won't thrive without it.

5. Solve Problems Together

There's no such thing as a smooth sailing relationship. Everyone encounters issues in their relationship, whether it be a friendship, business-relationship, or intimate relationship. Some of these issues might be quite minor when reflecting back on at a later time, while others can be more difficult to deal with. Problems faced in a relationship are all a test of one another's patience and it's up to them on how to solve them.

People who have strong connections with others and the more real friendships you develop, the more resilient you're going to be, because you have a strong support network to fall back on.

Resiliency in Dealing with Difficult People

In turbulent times, the need to build resilience in handling difficult people is greater than ever. While you cannot control another person's attitude or behaviors, it is important to remember that you can control your own. How you approach the challenge of dealing with difficult people can make all the difference in your own attitude and perspective. Dealing with difficult people is a continuing challenge in any setting, personal or business-related.

Possessing a mental toughness trait, comprising both the combination of resilience and confidence, can help you manage those people and those situations to your advantage. Mental toughness equips you with the calm and resolve to help you retain control of your emotions in potentially volatile situations. It also gives you the confidence and spirit to take on difficult people on your terms.

Some tools and techniques for managing difficult people include:

1. Stay Calm and Reasonable

Learning to stay calm and refraining from being provoked into a reaction is the first and most important piece of advice. Once the other person has provoked you into an emotional response, they have immediately gained the upper hand. Like many things, this is something to be learned over time and you will likely experience some trial and error here on exactly how you best achieve this, but once you have navigated a few such difficult situations successfully this will become much easier.

2. Emphasize then Respond, Don't React

Another benefit of staying calm and composed is that it enables you to proactively respond rather than negatively react. Feeling calm, in control, and acting from a position of strength rather than being uncontrollable and trying to recover from what was said or done, will help grant you the time to figure out the best way to handle an issue. One way to ensure that you respond rather than react is to put yourself in the shoes of the difficult person for a moment. By emphasizing with the person you can often diffuse the situation, as they then don't have any opposition to their case.

3. Put the Pressure Back on Them

Once you have emphasized with them, put the pressure back on them by calmly pushing for a solution. Difficult people have a tendency to make you feel uncomfortable or inadequate by putting you down and focusing on what they think you are doing wrong instead of being collaborative. If you can calmly and repeatedly ask them constructive questions about how best to solve the problem, you may disorientate them sufficiently to dissolve the situation.

4. Stick to the Facts

It can be difficult to stand your ground if you are being intimidated but, as much as you can, try not to cave into the pressure and stick to the facts. By thinking logically rather than emotionally, you can help diffuse the situation and focus on what's important. At all costs, it's important to avoid being drawn into an emotional reaction or bullying.

5. Pick Your Battles

This is as much a general as a specific piece of advice, but as much as its frustrating to pick your battles, the most efficient approach is to save your energy and mental anguish by walking away or avoiding the conflict altogether. Over time you'll learn which battles are worth picking a fight on, generally those that are most important to you on a matter of principle, and which you should leave well alone, such as those that are less important or outside your control.

Overall, mental toughness is a great trait to develop and most successful people have it because it helps them manage their day-to-day life, including dealing with difficult people.

Conclusion

If failure, difficulty, and suffering are unavoidable in life, then we need to prepare ourselves to face situations beyond our control, as the only thing we can fully control in life is ourselves. Therefore, we need to learn to be a person who has the capacity to adapt, recover, and continue to develop healthily when faced with difficult situations.

There will be times in all of our lives when pressures mount and at some points, we will struggle to cope. However, by learning about ourselves and realizing what we can and cannot control, we can manage, move on and make the most of life. Remember, your thinking and subsequent behavioral habits can create either bridges or barriers for a brighter future.

We have all had times when we have been stretched too thin, snapped, or felt broken. The concept of resilience, although complex, can be simplified as the metaphor of the rubber band. Rubber bands, just like people, come in various sizes and are subjected to different challenges, all while having different thicknesses and abilities to stretch.

If you stretch a rubber band to its maximum, it typically springs back thanks to its natural elasticity. We, too, have the ability to show more flexibility and spring back from life's challenges. Fortunately, we are not rubber bands. When we are stretched too thin, snap, or break, we simply don't end up in the trash! We can access help and get back on the right track.

To be on the right track, the ability to keep moving is essential. When you are not feeling confident, or things are not going your way, just move. Move out. Move on. Move up. Move smarter. Your ability to move will help you rise up from anything. You can completely recreate yourself and upgrade your circumstances. Nothing is permanent and you are not stuck.

By incorporating the tips learned within this book, you are sure to build the confidence to strengthen your resilience and successfully:

- View setbacks as impermanent,
- Manage your feelings and impulses,
- Focus on what you can control, &
- Cultivate embodied self-awareness.

Life always works out and with resilience, your mindset will allow you to see that things turn out in your favor, even if everything doesn't go according to the original plan. Find comfort in knowing that all you have and will experience is a transition and the transformation period that's leading you to bliss and abundance.

While focusing on the skills learned in this book, as well as the common characteristics of resilient people, you, too, can build and improve your resilience. Always believe that you can bend, endure any situation, and come out better than you were before.

As Jodi Picoult said:

"The human capacity for burden is like bamboo: far more flexible than you'd ever believe at first glance."

References

"7 Main Characteristics of a Resilient Person | No Barriers." No Barriers, 27 Aug. 2020, https://nobarriersusa.org/characteristics-resilient-person/.

"Achieving Resilience And Accepting Change | Spontaneous Happiness." DrWeil.Com, 9 Apr. 2018, https://www.drweil.com/blog/spontaneous-happiness/achieving-resilience-and-accepting-change/.

Ayub, Brisa Ayub. "How to Embrace Change with Resilience | Resilient Educator." ResilientEducator.Com, 9 Apr. 2020, https://resilienteducator.com/classroom-resources/embrace-change-with-resilience/.

B. Joelson DSW, LCSW, Richard B. "Locus of Control | Psychology Today." Psychology Today, 2 Aug. 2017, https://www.psychologytoday.com/us/blog/moments-matter/201708/locus-control.

"Building Your Resilience and Understanding Your Purpose - SmartCompany." SmartCompany, 9 Oct. 2017, https://www.smartcompany.com.au/people-human-resources/wellbeing/building-resilience-understanding-purpose/.

Burbe, Hert. "Internet for the Spirit." Reddit, https://www.reddit.com/r/wholesomememes/.

"Self-Compassion for Building Resilience - Emintell." Emintell, 5 Oct. 2020, https://www.emintell.com/self-compassion-for-building-resilience/.

Davis, Ph.D., Tchiki Davis, Ph. D. "Resilience 101: How to Be a More Resilient Person | Psychology Today." Psychology Today, 15 Mar. 2018, https://www.psychologytoday.com/us/blog/click-here-happiness/201803/resilience-101-how-be-more-resilient-person.

Fitzpatrick, Kevin. "Stephen Colbert's Outlook on Grief Moved Anderson Cooper to Tears | Vanity Fair." Vanity Fair,

Vanity Fair, 16 Aug. 2019,
https://www.vanityfair.com/hollywood/2019/08/colbert-
anderson-cooper-father-grief-tears.

G. Plante Ph.D., ABPP, Thomas G. Plante Ph. D., ABPP.
"Helping Others Offers Surprising Benefits | Psychology
Today." Psychology Today, 2 July 2012,
https://www.psychologytoday.com/us/blog/do-the-right-
thing/201207/helping-others-offers-surprising-benefits-0.

"Guest Blog: Four Ways to Build Resilience Using Positive
Thinking - Harvest HR." Harvest HR, 7 Mar. 2018,
https://www.harvesthr.com.au/2018/03/guest-blog-four-ways-
to-build-resilience-using-positive-thinking/.

"Guide to Coping with Change and Boosting Resilience |
CABA - The Charity Supporting Chartered Accountants'
Wellbeing." CABA - The Charity Supporting Chartered
Accountants' Wellbeing, 28 Jan. 2013,
https://www.caba.org.uk/help-and-guides/information/guide-
coping-change-and-boosting-resilience.

Guise, Stephen. "How to Be Resilient." Stephen Guise, 29
Aug. 2017, https://stephenguise.com/how-to-be-resilient/.

Hamby Ph.D., Sherry Hamby Ph. D. "Sense of Purpose—The
Most Important Strength? | Psychology Today." Psychology
Today, 31 Jan. 2020,
https://www.psychologytoday.com/us/blog/the-web-
violence/202001/sense-purpose-the-most-important-strength.

"How Finding Purpose Helps Build Your Resilience - Line
Hilton Vocal, Performance and Resilience Coach." Line
Hilton Vocal, Performance and Resilience Coach, 5 June
2020, https://www.linehilton.com/how-finding-purpose-helps-
build-your-resilience/.

Jacobs, Tom. "Evidence Mounts That Mindfulness Breeds
Resilience." Greater Good, 12 Oct. 2015,
https://greatergood.berkeley.edu/article/item/evidence_mounts
_that_mindfulness_breeds_resilience.

Jones, Meghan. "Tardigrades: The Most Indestructible Species
on the Planet." Reader's Digest, Reader's Digest, 11 Sept.

2017, https://www.readersdigest.ca/culture/tardigrades-indestructible-species/.

Knowledge, Maritime. "Building Resilience: Take Care of Yourself - SAFETY4SEA." SAFETY4SEA, 3 Oct. 2019, https://safety4sea.com/cm-building-resilience-take-care-of-yourself/.

Lipkin, Dr. Nicole. "The 8 Behaviors of Resilient People | by Dr. Nicole Lipkin | ThinkGrowth.Org." ThinkGrowth.Org, ThinkGrowth.org, 3 Nov. 2016, https://thinkgrowth.org/the-8-behaviors-of-resilient-people-a3d1acdeb8f1.

Lister, Nina-Marie Lister. "From Reactive to Proactive Resilience: Designing the New Sustainability – The Nature of Cities." The Nature of Cities, 15 Mar. 2016, https://www.thenatureofcities.com/2016/03/15/from-reactive-to-proactive-resilience-designing-the-new-sustainability/.

M. Schaefer, Stacey M. Schaefer, et al. "Purpose in Life Predicts Better Emotional Recovery from Negative Stimuli." PubMed Central (PMC), https://www.ncbi.nlm.nih.gov/pmc/articles/PMC3827458/.

Mind Life Project. "Building Resilience with Mindfulness - Mind Life Project." Mind Life Project, 26 Feb. 2019, https://mindlifeproject.com/managing-tough-times-with-mindfulness/.

Neill, James. "What Is Locus of Control." Https://Www.Usmcu.Edu, Dec. 2006, https://www.usmcu.edu/Portals/218/What%20is%20Locus%20of%20Control%20by%20James%20Neill.pdf.

Newman, Kira M. "Five Science-Backed Strategies to Build Resilience." Greater Good, 9 Nov. 2016, https://greatergood.berkeley.edu/article/item/five_science_backed_strategies_to_build_resilience.

Parker-Pope, Tara. "The Science of Helping Out - The New York Times." The New York Times - Breaking News, US News, World News and Videos, 9 Apr. 2020, https://www.nytimes.com/2020/04/09/well/mind/coronavirus-resilience-psychology-anxiety-stress-volunteering.html.

Patel, Deep. "8 Ways Successful People Master Resilience."
Ladders | Business News & Career Advice, TheLadders.com,
15 Mar. 2020, https://www.theladders.com/career-advice/8-
ways-successful-people-master-resilience.

Ribeiro, Lise. "Resilience: Learning Resilience from
Experience | Oasis." The Oasis School of Human Relations,
13 Dec. 2016,
https://www.oasishumanrelations.org.uk/blog/resilience-
learning-from-experience/.

Riley, Kaelyn. "How to Embrace Uncertainty - Experience
Life." Experience Life, 14 Dec. 2020,
https://experiencelife.com/article/how-to-embrace-
uncertainty/.

Shattell, Ph.D., RN, FAAN, Mona Shattell, Ph.D., RN,
FAAN, and Angela Johnson Johnson, Dipl OM, MSTOM,
MPH, LAc Dipl OM, MSTOM, MPH, LAc. "Mindful Self-
Compassion: How It Can Enhance Resilience." Healio:
Medical News, Journals, and Free CME, 12 Jan. 2018,
https://www.healio.com/psychiatry/journals/jpn/2018-1-56-
1/%7Be89ab10a-9170-4e0e-8fb7-
dae844e4c074%7D/mindful-self-compassion-how-it-can-
enhance-resilience.

"Mindful Self-Compassion: How It Can Enhance Resilience."
Healio: Medical News, Journals, and Free CME, 1 Dec. 2018,
https://www.healio.com/psychiatry/journals/jpn/2018-1-56-
1/%7Be89ab10a-9170-4e0e-8fb7-
dae844e4c074%7D/mindful-self-compassion-how-it-can-
enhance-resilience.

Sloan, Karlin Sloan. "Resilience : Helping Others Helps You."
LinkedIn.Com, 13 Oct. 2017,
https://www.linkedin.com/pulse/resilience-helping-others-
helps-you-karlin-sloan.

Smith, Ph.D., LPC, Kathleen Smith, Ph.D., LPC. "The
Psychology Of Dealing With Change: How to Become
Resilient." Psycom.Net - Mental Health Treatment Resource
Since 1996, https://www.psycom.net/dealing-with-change.

Stuever, Hank. "2019's Best TV Moment? It Was Stephen
Colbert Answering Anderson Cooper's Question about Grief.
- The Washington Post." Washington Post, The Washington
Post, 23 Dec. 2019,
https://www.washingtonpost.com/entertainment/tv/2019s-
best-tv-moment-it-was-stephen-colbert-answering-anderson-
coopers-question-about-grief/2019/12/23/ff7cec4e-236b-11ea-
a153-dce4b94e4249_story.html.

Suttie, Jill. "Four Ways Social Support Makes You More
Resilient." Greater Good, 17 Nov. 2017,
https://greatergood.berkeley.edu/article/item/four_ways_social
_support_makes_you_more_resilient.

Ungar Ph.D., Michael Ungar Ph. D. "Does Mindfulness Really
Make Us Resilient? | Psychology Today." Psychology Today,
3 Oct. 2015,
https://www.psychologytoday.com/us/blog/nurturing-
resilience/201510/does-mindfulness-really-make-us-resilient.

"Why Resilience and Positive Thinking Matters - BackupHR."
BackupHR, 23 Mar. 2020, https://www.backuphr.com/why-
resilience-and-positive-thinking-matters/.

Woodworth, James Woodworth. "What Are the
Characteristics of Resilient People and How to Develop Them
| Psychreg." Psychreg,
https://www.facebook.com/psychreg.org, 28 Oct. 2016,
https://www.psychreg.org/characteristics-of-resilient-people/.
Last updated on: 13 June 2020.

Kerig, P. (2020). Strengthening your resilience: Take care of
yourself as you care for others. Los Angeles, CA, and
Durham, NC: National Center for Child Traumatic Stress.

About The Author

Ashley M. Stephenson was born and raised in Northeast Ohio but was never content with staying in one place for long. That sense of wanderlust led her to Chicago, Illinois, Washington, D.C., and eventually to the lights and bustle of New York City.

She is a legal professional with over a decade of experience and who always rises to the next challenge.

Ashley's unique perspective for development inspires those around her. She is a member of several professional organizations, from the local Bar Associations, Mindfulness in Law Society,

Military Spouse J.D. Network, to the Alexander Hamilton Awareness Society.

Her creative side emerged after she began to understand how important wellness is to each of us. Her work has been featured in the Huffington Post and several legal industry magazines. Her passion for all she does has landed her speaking events at community colleges as well as societal groups in various cities.

An advocate for living a balanced lifestyle, Ashley spends much of her free time cultivating resilience. She enjoys traveling with her husband and is constantly in search of inspiration in those new and exotic locations she discovers. A woman on a quest for constant learning and growth, Ashley is a shining example for others to follow.